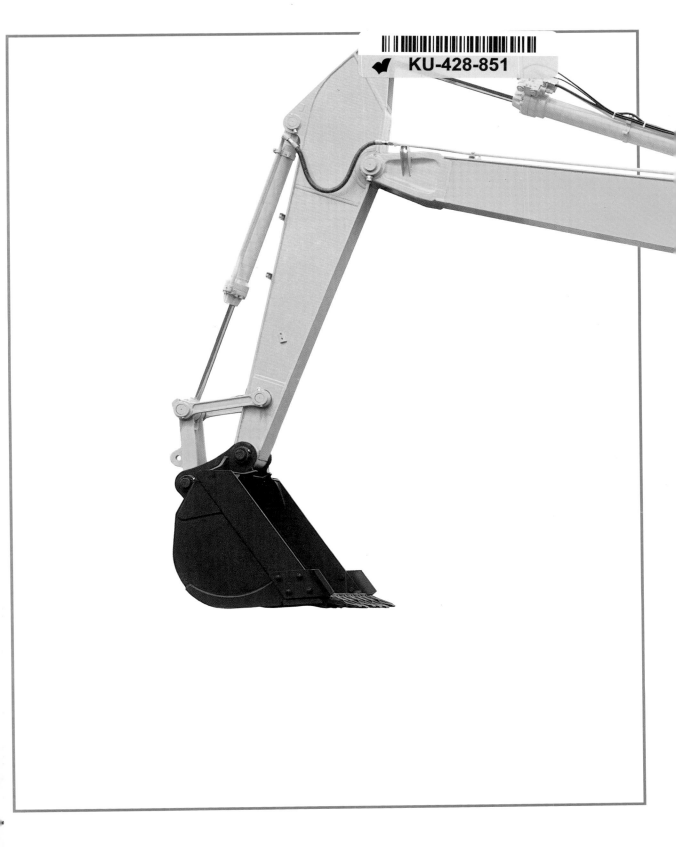

SNAP SHOT™

Senior Editor Mary Ling
Art Editor Joanna Pocock
Editor Caroline Bingham
Designers Sara Hill, Claire Penny
Production Catherine Semark

A Dorling Kindersley Book
First published in Great Britain in 1994
by Snapshot™, an imprint of Covent Garden Books
9 Henrietta Street, London WC2E 8PS

Copyright © 1994 Covent Garden Books Limited, London

Second printing 1994

Picture credits:- First Waste: 12/13; Terex: 14/15
Photography by Finbar Hawkins and Richard Leeney.
All rights reserved.

A CIP catalogue record for this book is
available from the British Library
ISBN 1-85948-020-9

Colour reproduction by Colourscan
Printed in Belgium by Proost

Diggers and Dumpers

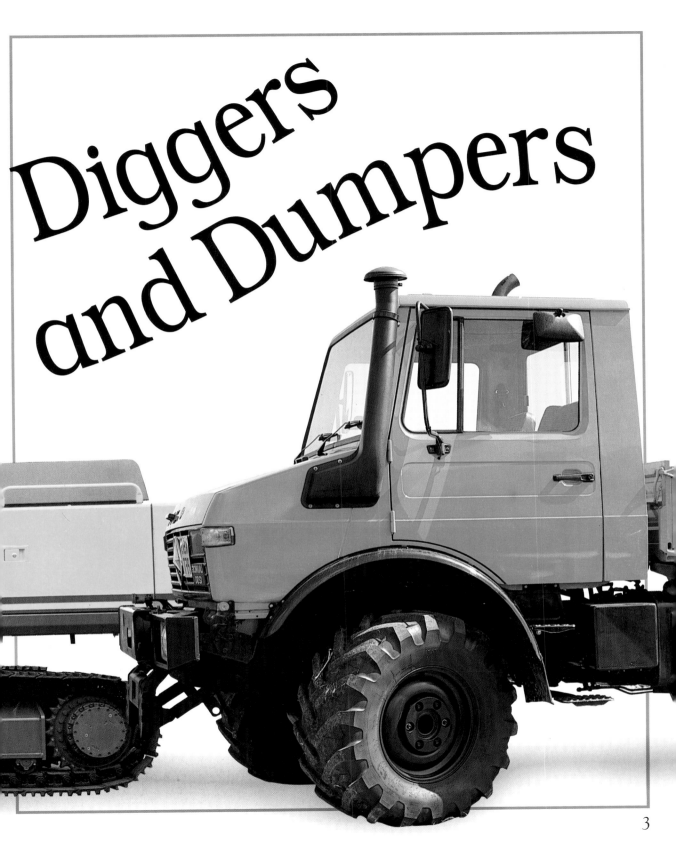

Contents

Multi-purpose
truck

Skid steer

What has sharp teeth and strong legs?

This excavator is ready to tear into the ground with its big toothy bucket. The sturdy legs next to the wheels keep the machine steady while it digs.

Wheeled excavator

Lift and carry with

Fork-lift truck

a fork!

It's easy to lift and stack heavy crates with machines like these. Crates are lifted by the strong steel forks, then the truck drives the cargo to its new place.

Dumper

4000

How do you empty a big bucket?

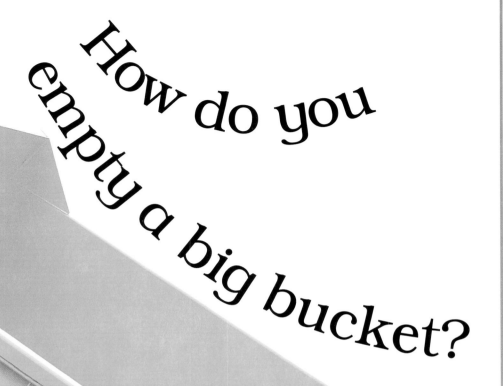

A dumper has a bucket, called a skip, that tips up and down. When the skip tilts up, the contents slide to the ground.

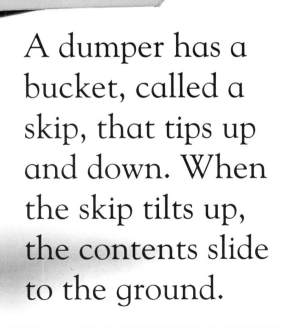

What happens to your rubbish?

Rubbish collection truck

Road sweeper

Rubbish is picked up and squashed into the back of a rubbish collection truck and taken to a dump. A road sweeper sucks litter off the streets.

How heavy is this rock?

This giant wheel loader is carrying a rock that is as heavy as three full-grown elephants. That's a very heavy load!

Giant wheel loader

Do machines ...

An excavator and a dump truck make a good team. The excavator uses its big shovel to fill the dump truck with earth, just like filling a wheelbarrow.

Track excavator

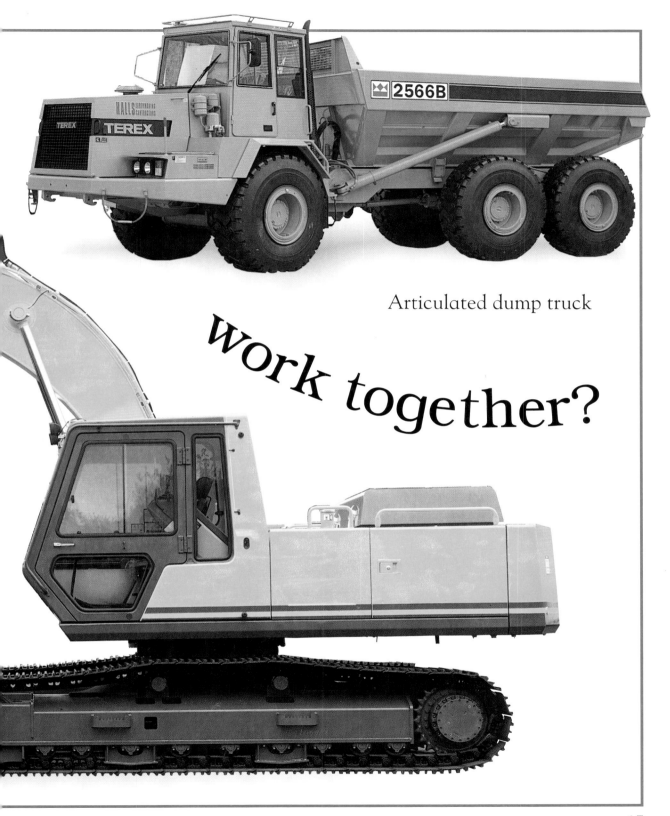

Articulated dump truck

work together?

Does a bulldozer

No! A bulldozer crawls along on ridged metal tracks that won't get stuck in muddy earth.

have wheels?

Bulldozer

Paver

A paver lays sticky
tarmac along the
path of a new
road. Then a
huge machine
called a roller
squashes down
the tarmac.

How are roads built?

Roller

HW 90

21

A backhoe loader can do two different jobs. It uses a back bucket to dig holes and a front shovel to clear away the dirt.

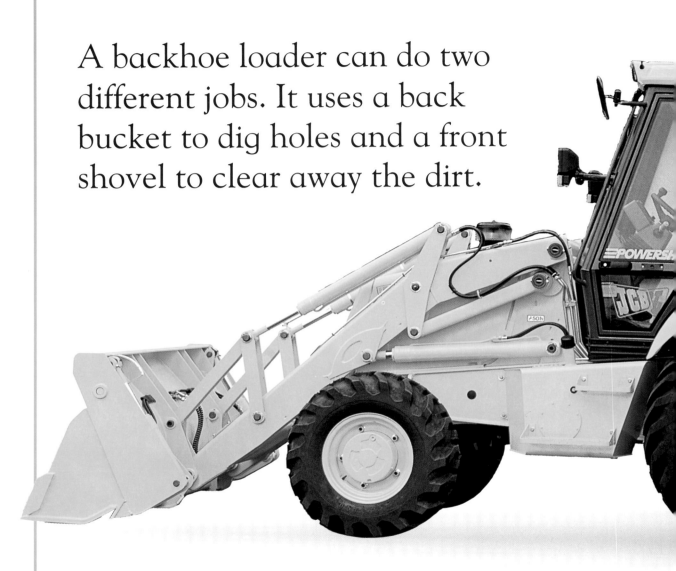

The front shovels ...

Backhoe loader

and the back digs

23

Tractor

What groovy tyres!

Tractor tyres have deep grooves
to help the tractor grip the earth
even when it's really muddy.

Ready to load

This useful truck has lots of space for carrying heavy things. Load up the back and off it goes.

Multi-purpose truck

Skid and steer

S60

Skid steer

Skid steers can shovel and carry things. They are often used instead of bigger machines because they can turn around in very small spaces.

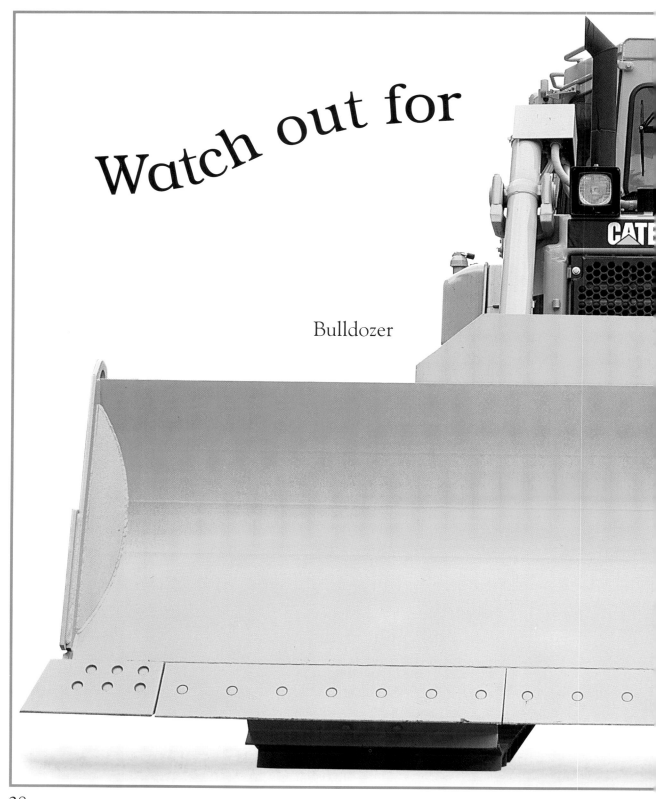

Watch out for

Bulldozer

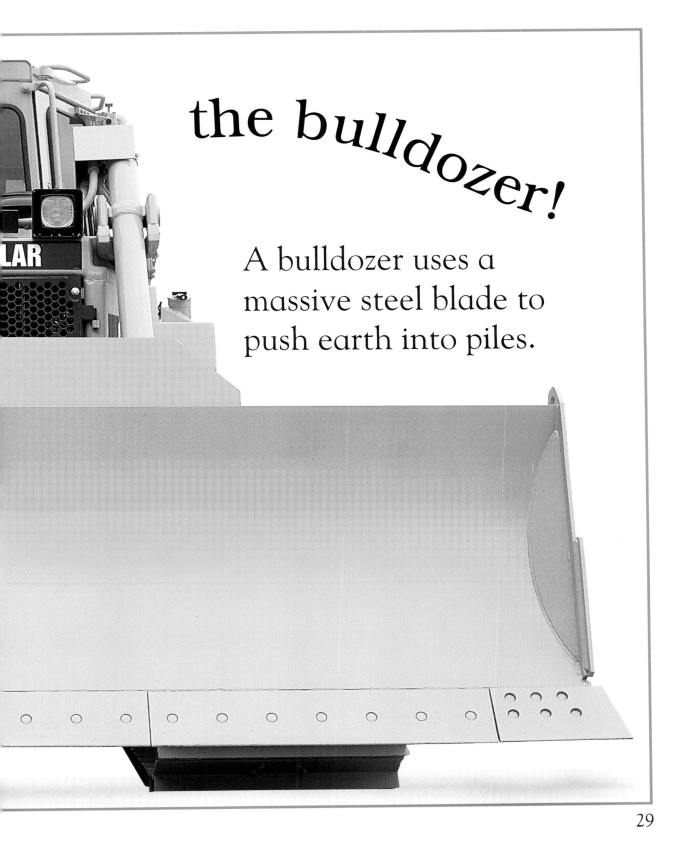

the bulldozer!

A bulldozer uses a massive steel blade to push earth into piles.

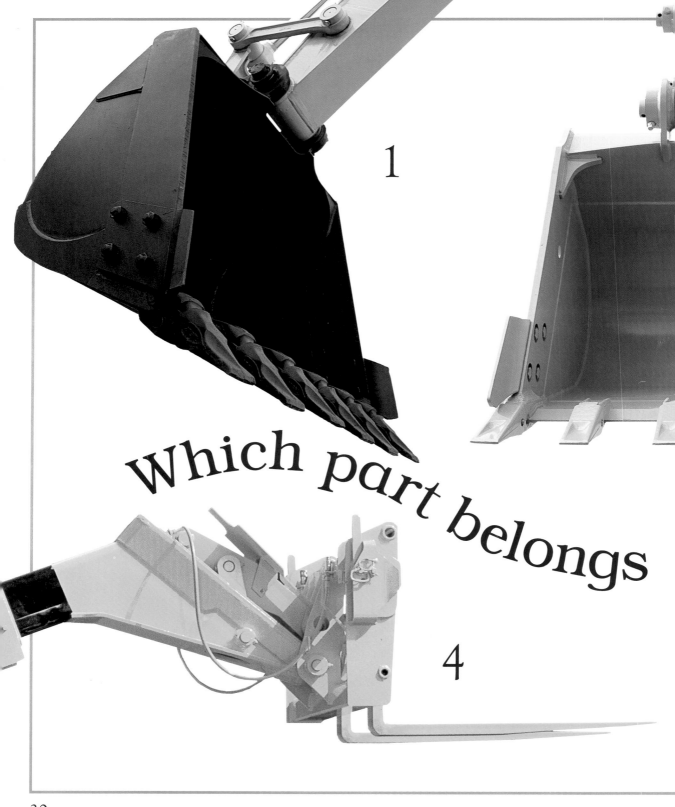

1

Which part belongs

4

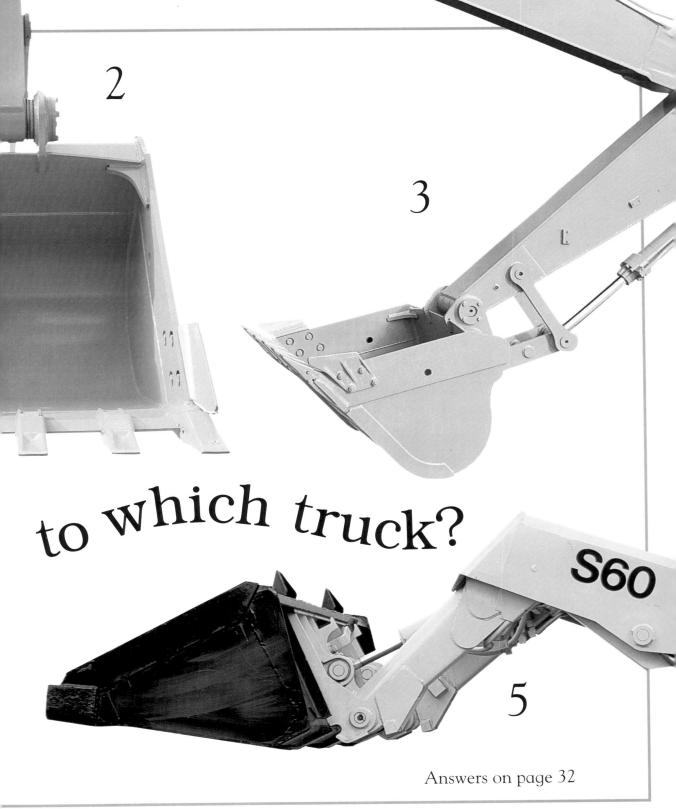

2

3

to which truck?

S60

5

Answers on page 32

Answers

1, 2, 3. Excavators
4. Telescopic handler
5. Skid steer